Rabbit walked and walked.
He saw footprints.
They were great big footprints.

"A giant has frightened everything away," said Rabbit.
"I will catch this giant."

How Rabbit Caught the Sun

One day, Rabbit said to his grandmother, "I am a good hunter. I am going hunting."

So Rabbit made a net.
He put the net in a tree.
But he did not catch the giant.

Rabbit said to his grandmother,
"Please, make a magic net
so I can catch this giant."

So his grandmother made
a magic net.
Rabbit put the net
between two trees.

In the morning,
Rabbit and Grandmother Rabbit
went to the net.
They saw what was in the net.
They were frightened.

"Let me out!" roared the sun.
"Let me out!"

"I can't!" shouted Rabbit.
"You're too hot!"

"Let him out!"
shouted Grandmother Rabbit.
She gave Rabbit a knife.

Rabbit cut the net.
The sun raced back to the sky.

To this day, Rabbit has
a mark on his back
where the sun burned his fur.